W9-DAD-707

Rosa Parks

by Jill C. Wheeler

visit us at
www.abdopub.com

Published by ABDO & Daughters, an imprint of ABDO
Publishing Company, 4940 Viking Drive, Suite 622, Edina,
Minnesota 55435. Copyright ©2003 by Abdo Consulting
Group, Inc. International copyrights reserved in all countries.
No part of this book may be reproduced in any form without
written permission from the publisher.

Printed in the United States.

Edited by Paul Joseph
Graphic Design: John Hamilton
Cover Design: Mighty Media
Interior Photos: AP/Photo, p. 5, 17, 23, 36, 37, 38, 41, 43, 45,
52, 61
Corbis, p. 1, 7, 8, 11, 13, 15, 18, 19, 20, 25, 27, 29, 30, 33, 35,
46, 49, 51, 53, 55, 57, 60

Library of Congress Cataloging-in-Publication Data

Wheeler, Jill C., 1964-
    Rosa Parks / Jill C. Wheeler.
        p. cm. — (Breaking barriers)
    Includes index.
    Summary: A biography of the African-American woman and civil
rights worker whose refusal to give up her seat on a bus led to a boycott
which lasted more than a year in Montgomery, Alabama.
    ISBN 1-57765-640-7
    1. Parks, Rosa, 1913- —Juvenile literature. 2. African-American
women—Alabama—Montgomery—Biography—Juvenile literature.
3. African-Americans—Alabama—Montgomery—Biography—
Juvenile literature. 4. Civil rights workers—Alabama—Montgomery—
Biography—Juvenile literature. 5. Montgomery (Ala.)—Biography—
Juvenile literature. 6. African-Americans—Civil rights—Alabama—
Montgomery—History—20th century—Juvenile literature.
7. Segregation in transportation—Alabama—Montgomery—Juvenile
literature. 8. Montgomery (Ala.)—Race relations—Juvenile literature.
[1. Parks, Rosa, 1913- 2. Civil rights workers. 3. African-Americans—Biography. 4. Women—Biography.] I. Title.

F334.M753 P379 2002
323'.092—dc21
[B]
                                                    2001027938

Contents

A Legacy of Freedom

A throng of photographers and admirers crowded around the large, white limousine as it pulled up to the Garfield Community Center in Seattle, Washington. Cameras flashed as the door opened and a small, white-haired woman stepped out. The woman smiled and waved as she made her way inside.

During her childhood in Alabama, she had lived a much different lifestyle. She was an African-American. In those days, most white people considered black people to be inferior. She had to fight against laws that treated African-Americans as second-class citizens. As a result, she had to struggle to get an education. She also had difficulty registering to vote.

The woman was Rosa Parks. Forty years earlier, she could not afford a car. Now she was 83 years old and traveling by limousine on a 40-city tour. She and other African-Americans were telling their life stories.

Around the country, people of all ages listened as Parks and her friends told of their struggles for

Rosa Parks

equality. Parks recounted moments that changed her life and the lives of millions of others.

Parks and her group called themselves the Parks Legacy Team. They were on the road for 381 days. That was exactly how long the Montgomery bus boycott had lasted 40 years earlier. Parks had ignited the famous boycott when she refused to give up her seat on a public bus to a white man.

Wherever the Parks Legacy Team went, it encouraged people to continue the fight for equality. "I know we have made some progress over the years," Parks told her audience in Seattle. "But I know we also have to continue."

Grandma and Grandpa's Farm

*R*osa Louise McCauley was born on February 4, 1913, in Tuskegee, Alabama. She was the first child of Leona Edwards McCauley and James McCauley. Rosa's mother was a teacher. Her father was a carpenter. His work building houses took him all over Alabama.

As a child, Rosa was often sick. She battled tonsillitis throughout her childhood. Leona had a difficult time caring for Rosa when James was away working. So when Rosa was a toddler, she and her mother moved. They went to live with Leona's parents on their farm in Pine Level, Alabama.

Shortly afterward, Rosa's brother, Sylvester, was born. Rosa's father came to live with them at the farm for a while. Then he left to do more carpentry work. He was gone for two and a half years. He returned for several days when Rosa was five, and then left once more. Rosa didn't see him again until she was an adult.

Children picking cotton during the fall harvest in Pulaski County, Arkansas, 1935.

Rosa enjoyed living with her grandparents, Sylvester and Rose Edwards. They told her many stories about her family on her mother's side. Grandpa Sylvester had light skin because his father was a white plantation owner. Grandpa Sylvester's parents both died when he was young. The plantation overseer raised him and treated him very poorly. Rosa's grandfather never forgot how horrible his childhood had been. He taught his family to never put up with bad treatment from anyone. He encouraged them to become educated so they would never have to cook or clean for white people.

A school for black children in Tuskegee, Alabama, 1902.

Leona had listened to her father and earned a teaching certificate. She returned to teaching after Rosa's brother was born. At that time, black teachers were allowed to teach only black children. There were few schools for black children, so Leona had to travel quite a distance to teach. Because she didn't have a car, she had to stay at the school all week, returning home only on weekends. Rosa's grandfather took Leona to school and back in his mule-drawn wagon.

When her mother was gone, Rosa loved to go fishing with her grandparents. They were getting older, so they often asked Rosa to help them bait their hooks with plump, wriggling worms. She also helped her grandparents on their farm, where they grew vegetables and raised chickens. Unlike many other blacks in the area, the Edwards family owned its land.

Rosa and her brother attended the local one-room school. The school was a small, wooden building near the African-American church. Fifty to 60 students in first grade through sixth grade all sat in the same room, with just one teacher. The schools for the white children were larger and made of brick.

Rosa and her brother had to walk to school. White children had school buses to ride. Sometimes the school buses rumbled past Rosa as she walked to school. The white children would throw garbage out the bus windows at her and the other black children.

When Rosa grew older, she learned that the schools for white children were built and heated with money from taxpayers. That money came from both white and black taxpayers. Despite this, the black community had to build its own schools and heat them without any help from tax money.

The white schools held classes for nine months each year. The black schools held classes for just five months. This allowed black children to work in the fields during the busy harvest times. Rosa worked in the fields, too. After she helped her grandparents, she worked on a nearby farm owned by whites. She started working in the cotton fields when she was about six years old.

Rosa and her family worked from sunrise to sunset. Each person received 50 cents a day for chopping cotton, and one dollar for each 100 pounds of cotton he or she picked. "I never will forget how the sun just burned into me," Parks recalled about her work in the fields. "The hot sand burned our feet whether or not we had our old work shoes on."

African-American children working in a cotton field.

Nights of Fear

*P*ine Level was a small town. In most larger towns in the South, public facilities such as drinking fountains and restrooms had signs marking them as "Colored" or "White." *Colored* was the term that people used in those days to describe African-Americans. Rosa never saw such things in Pine Level. Still, she felt the sting of segregation and discrimination. Some white people treated her nicely. Most white people, however, treated her and other black people without respect. The white children were mean too, because they had learned it from their parents.

Some white people truly hated black people. They believed white people were better than black people. They did not want their society to change, so they did not want black people to have rights. Many of these people joined an organization called the Ku Klux Klan (KKK). A group of Confederate soldiers had started the original form of the KKK after the U.S. Civil War. KKK members wore white robes and put white sheets over their faces so people didn't know who they were. Then they terrorized African-Americans with bombings, whippings, and shootings. They burned African-American churches and killed African-American people for virtually any reason.

Ku Klux Klan members salute a burning cross at a rally near New Orleans, Louisiana.

Lynchings were also common in those days. At a lynching, a group of white men beat, hanged, burned alive, or shot black people. The white men considered themselves to be carrying out justice, though there was never a trial to determine if the black person was guilty or innocent of a crime. Often the victims were innocent. African-American men were lynched simply for talking to white women. African-Americans were also lynched for attempting to vote. It didn't matter to the attackers that the U.S. Constitution gave African-Americans the right to vote.

Between 1900 and 1920, whites in the South lynched more than 1,000 African-Americans. The violence increased after World War I ended in 1918. Many African-American men had fought for their country in the war. They believed their country should treat them better in return. "The whites didn't like blacks having that kind of attitude," Parks remembered of the time. "So they started doing all kinds of violent things to black people to remind them that they didn't have any rights."

Rosa never forgot that frightening time after the war. Her grandfather would sit up at night with his shotgun at his side in case the KKK broke into their home. Fortunately they never did. Other blacks, however, were not so lucky.

An African-American becomes the victim of a lynch mob.

Separate and Unequal

*W*hen Rosa was 11, Leona sent her to a new school in Montgomery, Alabama. Back then, rural black schools only went through the sixth grade. Any black child who wanted to go to junior high school or high school had to go to the city.

The school Rosa attended was called the Montgomery Industrial School. A group of white women from the North ran the school. The principal and cofounder was Miss Alice White. Everyone called the school Miss White's school.

Not everyone agreed with Miss White's belief in educating African-Americans. Several times, people burned down the school. Miss White always rebuilt it. And because the white teachers were teaching black students, most white people wouldn't talk to them. Miss White and her staff found their friends within the African-American community instead.

A boy peers through the fence around the jail yard in Birmingham, Alabama, after he was arrested with hundreds of others for marching in an anti-segregation demonstration in 1963.

Rosa enjoyed Miss White's school. She studied English, science, geography, and domestic science. Domestic science included classes in cooking, sewing, and caring for sick people. She learned things that weren't in textbooks, as well. "What I learned best at Miss White's school was that I was a person with dignity and self-respect," Parks remembered. "And I should not set my sights lower than anybody else just because I was black. I had learned it from my grandparents and my mother, too."

African-American children attend a segregated elementary school in Washington, D.C., in 1942.

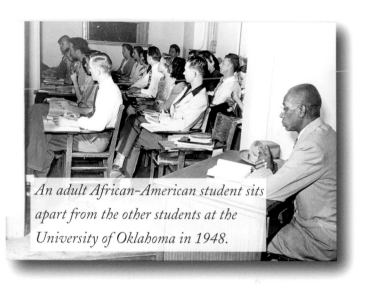

An adult African-American student sits apart from the other students at the University of Oklahoma in 1948.

In Montgomery, Rosa came face to face with the harsh realities of segregation. Segregation was a way of life in the South at the time. It originated when slavery was still legal. Even after slavery was abolished following the Civil War, many white people did not want things to change. In the early 1900s, many southern states created entirely separate societies for whites and blacks.

Segregation laws touched nearly every part of daily life for blacks living in the South. For example, Louisiana had a law that required all circuses to have separate entrances for blacks and whites. A Kentucky law stated that no schoolbook used by a black child could ever be used by a white child, and the other way around. Rosa's home state of Alabama even had a law that prohibited black people and white people from playing checkers together.

In Montgomery, Rosa found drinking fountains and restrooms marked "Colored" or "White." But segregation went far beyond drinking fountains and restrooms. In the South, every school, restaurant, train car, hotel, and waiting room was segregated. So was every swimming pool, hospital, elevator, and prison. Whites and blacks had separate churches. Even in courtrooms, blacks swore to tell the truth on one Bible, and whites swore on another one.

A segregated drinking fountain in the South.

FOR COLORED ONLY

As Rosa learned to get by in segregated society, she continued her studies. Rosa had completed the eighth grade when Miss White's school closed. Miss White was ready to retire by then. She couldn't find anyone to take over running the school. Rosa transferred to Montgomery's only black public junior high school, Booker T. Washington Junior High, for ninth grade.

For tenth and eleventh grades, Rosa attended the laboratory school at Alabama State Teachers' College for Negroes. The laboratory school gave student teachers at the college a chance to practice their skills.

Rosa never finished eleventh grade. That fall, her grandmother Rose became sick. Rosa dropped out of school to take care of her. A month later, her grandmother died. Rosa returned to school later only to have to leave again when her mother became ill. "I was not happy about dropping out of school either time," she said. "But it was my responsibility to help with my grandmother, and later to take care of my mother. I did not complain; it was just something that had to be done."

Wedding Bells

Rosa now was responsible for taking care of her grandparents' farm. She also worked for a while in a shirt factory and did domestic work. *Domestic work* was the term for helping with cleaning and cooking in white people's homes.

When Rosa was 18 years old, a friend introduced her to a young man named Raymond Parks. The 28-year-old was a barber in Montgomery. Rosa had a polite conversation with him, and then forgot about him. But Raymond didn't forget about Rosa.

One day, someone in a sporty, red car with a rumble seat came driving down the road near Rosa's farm. It was Raymond. He had asked around until he found out where she lived. Rosa refused to spend much time with him at first. As she got to know him, though, she realized that she loved talking with him. Like Rosa's grandfather, Raymond had light skin. Many people thought he was white. Like Rosa, he had been raised to stand up for himself. He told many interesting stories about growing up in an all-white neighborhood and passing for a white person.

"I was very impressed by the fact that he didn't seem to have that meek attitude . . . toward white people," Parks recalled. "I thought he was a very nice

Rosa Parks at a Detroit news conference in 1998.

man, an interesting man who talked very intelligently. He could talk for hours at a time about all the things he had lived through."

Raymond was also the first activist that Rosa had ever met. Raymond was a member of the National Association for the Advancement of Colored People (NAACP). When Rosa met Raymond, he was raising money to defend nine young African-Americans known as the Scottsboro Boys. The young men had been convicted of attacking two white women. All but the youngest, a 12-year-old boy, had been sentenced to death for the crime. This was despite evidence of their innocence presented during the trial. The NAACP helped them appeal their case.

In August 1932, Raymond asked Leona if he could marry Rosa. She agreed, and on December 18, 1932, Rosa and Raymond Parks got married at Rosa's home in Pine Level. The newlyweds moved to Montgomery, and Rosa went back to school and earned her high school diploma. That made her one of only a handful of blacks in Montgomery who had a high school education. Even seven years later, only seven out of every 100 blacks had a high school diploma.

Even with a diploma, Rosa had few employment options. For a while, she worked as a helper in a hospital. She took in sewing projects on the side to make extra money. Then she got a job at the local Army Air Force base. Meanwhile, her husband continued to work to help the Scottsboro Boys. Often, that involved secret meetings.

Rosa worried whenever her husband went to his meetings. She knew that many white people wanted to find men like Raymond who were helping black people. "Every time he was at those meetings with those people, I wondered if he would come back alive," she said. She was always relieved when he came home. Raymond didn't tell her much about what went on at his meetings. That way, if anyone questioned her, she could honestly say she didn't know.

The new trials and appeals in the Scottsboro case went on for years. The original trial had begun in 1931. Eight of the defendants were finally released over the course of the next two decades, while the ninth escaped from prison in 1948. "I was proud of [Raymond] for working on behalf of the Scottsboro Boys," Rosa said. "I also admired his courage. He could have been beaten or killed for what he was doing."

These are nine African-Americans accused in the Scottsboro case. Fearing a mob lynching, Alabama Governor B.M. Miller called the National Guard to the Scottsboro jail for extra security.

On a Mission to Vote

*W*hen the Scottsboro Boys were saved from execution, Parks's husband turned his efforts to another issue. That issue was registering African-Americans to vote. The Fifteenth Amendment granted African-Americans the right to vote after the Civil War. Despite this, the southern states created rules that made it nearly impossible for blacks to exercise that right. They prevented blacks from voting primarily by making it difficult for them to register. One rule was that black people had to have white people vouch for them if they wanted to register. They also had to take a special literacy test to show that they understood the U.S. Constitution. And they had to pay a poll tax.

Parks's husband got help in his quest from an African-American lawyer named Arthur Madison. Madison worked with a group of blacks in Montgomery, including Parks and her husband. He helped them register to vote.

An African-American woman swears an oath as she registers to vote in Alabama.

Parks first tried to register to vote in 1943. It was challenging. Blacks could only register at certain times, and those times never were publicized. African-Americans had to call and ask when they could come to register. Often those times were during regular working hours. That was done to discourage blacks from registering. If a black person did take time off from work to come, the line of people waiting to register was often long. The workers who registered voters closed the office at the end of the designated time. It didn't matter to them if there was still a long line of people waiting to register when they closed.

The first time Parks tried to register, she didn't receive her voter's certificate in the mail. The second time she tried, the registration workers told her she did not pass, but they did not tell her why. Parks was quite sure she had passed the test. But the registration workers could lie about test scores if they wanted, and no one would ever know.

Parks took the voter registration test for a third time in 1945. She made a copy of her answers to the 21 questions just in case she didn't receive her voter's certificate in the mail. Fortunately, she received it this time. Next, she had to pay the poll tax.

Many African-Americans endured long lines as they waited to register to vote.

African-Americans in Mississippi vote for the first time since 1890 in the 1946 Democratic primary.

The poll tax was another rule whites made to keep blacks from voting. When Parks registered, the poll tax was $1.50 per year. Voters were supposed to pay the tax each year they could vote. The voting age back then was 21. Voters who registered at age 21 had to pay $1.50 each year from then on for as long as they wanted to vote.

The poll tax was retroactive. That meant that if people first registered to vote after age 21, they had to pay poll taxes back to when they turned 21. That could add up to a lot of money. White people were not denied voting registration, so they could register right when they turned 21. And since they didn't have to pay the retroactive poll tax, they didn't have to come up with a lot of money at once. Parks had no choice but to pay the poll tax.

Parks worked to help other African-Americans register to vote. She also joined the NAACP and volunteered as the secretary for the local chapter. As secretary, she took notes at the meetings. She also helped the NAACP officials work with African-Americans who had been the victims of violence, discrimination, or poor treatment.

Time after time, Parks and the NAACP officials heard from African-Americans who had been unjustly accused, abused, or hurt. But African-Americans weren't the only ones. Some white people spoke out against segregation and were often hurt, too. Parks noticed that the number of cases grew after World War II. As in World War I, African-American soldiers served their country. When they returned, they felt they should be treated better. Once again, most whites didn't want anything to change.

"I remember 1949 as a very bad year," Parks recalled. "Things happened that most people never heard about, because they never were reported in the newspapers. At times I felt overwhelmed by all the violence and hatred, but there was nothing to do but keep going."

Outside Alabama, the struggle against segregation was slowly pressing forward. One key issue was the segregation of public education. Civil rights workers won a significant battle in May 1954 with the U.S. Supreme Court ruling in *Brown v. Board of Education of Topeka, Kansas*. In the ruling, the court said that separate education could not be equal. The ruling paved the way for desegregation of public schools. By 1955, African-Americans were still waiting to see how the ruling would affect their local school system. But there were other pressing problems. Among the largest for Parks and other African-Americans in Montgomery was their treatment on public buses.

An elderly black woman holds a sample voting ballot during a class for newly registered voters in Alabama.

"You May Do That"

"*I* don't think any segregation law angered black people in Montgomery more than bus segregation," Parks recalled. "It was very humiliating having to suffer the indignity of riding segregated buses twice a day, five days a week, to go downtown and work for white people."

On Montgomery public buses, the first 10 seats were reserved for whites. African-Americans had to sit in the back seats of the bus. If the white seats filled up, bus drivers could demand that black passengers give away their seats to white passengers. Because blacks and whites were not allowed to sit in the same row, just one new white passenger meant four black passengers had to give up their seats. If the back seats were filled, blacks had to stand even if there were empty seats in the front of the bus. Blacks also had to enter the bus through the back door. They could go in the front door to pay their fare, but then they had to exit and re-enter the bus through the back door.

A segregated bus in Texas in 1956.

Parks had her own problems with the bus system. When she went to register to vote the second time, a white driver forced her off the bus for refusing to enter through the back door. "I didn't want to pay my fare and then go around to the back door, because many times, even if you did that, you might not get on the bus at all," she said. "They'd probably shut the door, drive off, and leave you standing there."

She never forgot how rudely she had been treated that time. She also never forgot the face of that angry bus driver. After that, she learned to look at the bus drivers. She wouldn't get on the bus if she saw the driver who had been mean to her before.

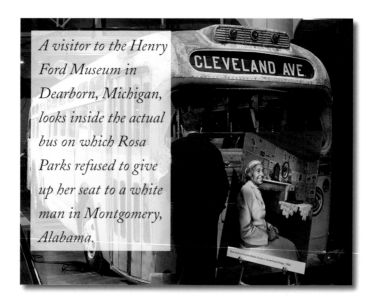

A visitor to the Henry Ford Museum in Dearborn, Michigan, looks inside the actual bus on which Rosa Parks refused to give up her seat to a white man in Montgomery, Alabama.

Rosa Parks sits in a 1950s-era bus in Montgomery, Alabama, in 1995, some 40 years after being arrested for refusing to give up her seat on a city bus to a white person.

On Thursday, December 1, 1955, Parks was on her way home from her tailoring job at the Montgomery Fair department store. As usual, she boarded the Cleveland Avenue bus and took a seat in the first row of the section for African-Americans. Too late, she realized that the driver was the same one who had forced her off the bus 12 years earlier.

At the next stop, a group of white people got on the bus. All of them got seats except one. The driver looked back at the African-American section of the bus. "Let me have those front seats," he said. At first, no one moved. The driver said, "Y'all better make it light on yourselves and let me have those seats." This time, the man next to Parks stood up. The two women sitting across the aisle from Parks stood as well. Parks slid over to the window seat that the man next to her had vacated. And she stayed seated.

Rosa Parks is fingerprinted in Montgomery, Alabama, on February 22, 1956, after her arrest for violating the state's segregation laws.

The driver then asked Parks if she was going to give up her seat. She said no. "I'm going to have you arrested," he said. "You may do that," Parks replied calmly.

Later, Parks recalled the thoughts that were going through her mind. "I kept thinking about my mother and my grandparents, and how strong they were," she said. "I knew there was a possibility of being mistreated, but an opportunity was being given to me to do what I had asked of others."

It wasn't long before two policemen arrived. One looked at Parks and asked her why she didn't give up her seat. She asked, "Why do you all push us around?" He replied, "I don't know, but the law is the law and you're under arrest."

In later years, many people thought that Parks wouldn't give up her seat because she was physically tired. She later explained, "The only tired I was, was tired of giving in."

Boycott!

*P*arks was not the first African-American to be arrested for refusing to obey the segregation laws on the buses. Earlier that year, two other women had been arrested for the same violation. Both times, the NAACP considered using their cases to change how black people were treated on the buses. However, neither situation had been ideal. With Parks, they knew immediately that they had found the perfect plaintiff. No one could say anything bad about Parks's character. She had a stable marriage, and she didn't have a police record. She was educated and had worked all her life. Parks agreed to let the NAACP use her arrest to get the laws changed.

Parks's friends paid her bail and got her out of jail that evening. Her trial was set for the following Monday. Over the weekend, a group of African-American leaders in Montgomery organized a black boycott of the public bus system for Monday. The boycott would protest segregation on the buses. Since 70 percent of the people who rode the buses were African-American, they knew the bus company would feel the economic pinch of such a boycott.

A bus in Montgomery, Alabama, sits empty.

By Friday evening, the group had put together flyers asking African-Americans not to ride the public buses on Monday. The group also asked the ministers of Montgomery's African-American churches to talk about the boycott during their Sunday services.

Monday, December 5, was overcast and dark. Still, when the Montgomery public buses rumbled by, they were nearly empty. Virtually all African-Americans in Montgomery had chosen to observe the boycott!

That morning, Parks went to the courthouse for her trial. To no one's surprise, the court found her guilty of breaking the segregation laws. They fined her $10, plus $4 in court costs. Parks's lawyers knew the only way to change the segregation laws was to force the issue in a higher court.

That evening, Parks attended a meeting at Holt Street Baptist Church. A group of black activists who had formed a new organization that day put on the meeting. They called their organization the Montgomery Improvement Association (MIA). They appointed a young minister, who had recently moved to Montgomery, as their president. His name was Dr. Martin Luther King, Jr.

Holt Street Baptist Church was packed. Organizers had to set up speakers outside the church so everyone who came could hear. The meeting's purpose was to decide if the bus boycott should continue. By the end of the evening, the audience voted overwhelmingly to continue staying off the buses. The Montgomery bus boycott had begun.

Rosa Parks is escorted to the Montgomery, Alabama, courthouse.

We Shall Overcome

"*N*o one had any idea how long it would last," Parks said of the boycott. "Some people said it couldn't last, but it seemed like those who said that were the white people and not us. The whites did everything they could do to stop it."

On the first day of the boycott, organizers worked with Montgomery's 18 African-American-owned taxi companies to arrange for reduced-fare rides for people who normally took the bus. Blacks who owned cars also volunteered to shuttle other blacks to work and back. As the boycott continued, the African-American churches purchased station wagons and operated them to give people rides. Some white employers even drove their black employees to and from work because they didn't want to lose them. Those who could walk to work walked, sometimes for miles.

Rosa Parks at the dedication of Rosa Parks Elementary School in San Francisco, California, on April 24, 1997.

Rosa Parks speaks with reporters as she arrives at court with Reverend Edward Nixon and 91 other African-Americans on trial for violating a 1921 anti-boycott law.

The white establishment fought back in any way it could. White people threatened to arrest cab drivers who charged less than full fare. They harassed groups of African-Americans waiting at bus stops for cabs or cars to pick them up. They refused to insure the churches' vehicles used to transport blacks. They arrested black drivers for even the smallest traffic violations.

The black community met each new restriction with determination and ingenuity. Some blacks volunteered to drive cabs when other drivers were arrested. A black insurance agent worked with Lloyds of London in England to insure the churches' station wagons. Organizers set up a complex system to direct the private cars and cabs to people who needed rides. By working together, the African-American community transported 30,000 people to work and back each day.

In spite of this system, many blacks lost their jobs during the boycott. Parks and her husband were among them. Parks isn't sure if losing her job was due to the boycott.

Meanwhile, the MIA had met with city leaders and the bus company to ask that blacks receive better treatment on the buses. The bus company refused to make any changes. Montgomery blacks had no choice but to continue the boycott.

In February 1956, Montgomery quit running the public buses. Only a handful of whites still rode the buses, so the bus company lost money each day. Downtown Montgomery businesses complained, as well, that the boycott cost them money. Whites owned most of the businesses, and blacks no longer did business with them.

By June, Parks's appeal had made its way to a federal district court. The court ruled in favor of Parks. The city of Montgomery then appealed that decision to the U.S. Supreme Court. In November 1956, the Supreme Court ruled that segregation on Montgomery buses was unconstitutional. Montgomery's African-American community had won a major victory in the fight for civil rights.

When the Supreme Court order arrived in December, the boycott ended. Montgomery's buses were legally integrated beginning December 21, 1956. That day, a team of photographers from *Look* magazine took Parks's picture. The famous photograph came to be a symbol of the U.S. Civil Rights movement.

Rosa Parks smiles as she walks on a street in Montgomery, Alabama, on December 21, 1956, the day a U.S. Supreme Court ruling took effect, banning segregation on the city's buses.

A Revolution Takes Hold

*M*ontgomery's successful bus boycott had shown how the African-American community could cause change by working together. African-Americans in other cities throughout the South began their own boycotts and nonviolent protests against segregation. One by one, the laws that treated blacks as second-class citizens began to change.

Millions of people around the country regarded Parks as a heroine. In Montgomery, however, the white establishment saw her as the troublemaker. Parks and her family had received threatening phone calls throughout the boycott. The calls continued after the buses were desegregated. Parks, her husband, and her mother decided to move to Detroit, Michigan, where Parks's brother Sylvester lived.

Parks had begun traveling nationally on behalf of civil rights during the bus boycott. She continued her travels after moving to Detroit. Martin Luther King, Jr., had become more involved than ever in the struggle for civil rights.

Dr. Martin Luther King, Jr.

King continued to use nonviolent methods of protest to raise awareness and work for change. Parks often accompanied him on marches or demonstrations. She was there to hear King's famous "I Have a Dream" speech during the 1963 March on Washington.

"The Civil Rights movement was having a big effect," Parks remembered. "It didn't change the

President Lyndon B. Johnson reaches to shake hands with Dr. Martin Luther King, Jr., after signing the Civil Rights Act of 1964.

Students in Montgomery, Alabama, protest a 1963 Supreme Court ruling to desegregate their schools.

hearts and minds of many white southerners, but it did make a difference to the politicians in Washington, D.C." In 1964, President Lyndon Johnson signed the Civil Rights Act. It was the most far-reaching civil rights legislation since right after the Civil War.

Parks returned to Alabama in March 1965, to take part in the 50-mile march from Selma to Montgomery. Organizers held the march to call attention to the problems in Selma. Officials there still made it difficult for African-Americans to register to vote. In August 1965, President Johnson signed the Voting Rights Act into law. It allowed African-Americans to register to vote with federal examiners if they were denied registration locally. The act was another major victory for blacks in the struggle for civil rights.

Moving On

*I*n 1965, Parks joined the staff of U.S. Representative John Conyers, Jr. He was an African-American from Michigan. Parks worked in his Detroit office as a receptionist and office assistant for more than 20 years. When she had been there three years, she heard the news that Martin Luther King, Jr., had been assassinated. She and her mother cried over the loss of a good friend and a powerful activist for freedom. Years later, Parks helped Conyers work to make Martin Luther King, Jr., Day a national holiday.

Sadly, Parks's losses didn't end there. Her husband, mother, and brother all became sick at the same time. Parks had to travel among three different hospitals to see them. In 1977, Parks's husband died of cancer. Three months later, Parks's brother also died of cancer. And finally, Parks's mother died of cancer two years later.

In February 1987, Parks founded the Rosa and Raymond Parks Institute for Self Development. She did this in memory of her husband and all his work for civil rights. The Institute primarily works to help young people reach their goals. Institute programs stress the values that Parks and her husband demonstrated during their years as activists. Those values include pride, courage, and discipline. Parks refers to the combination as "quiet strength."

Dr. Martin Luther King, Jr., stands with Rosa Parks at a dinner given in her honor in Birmingham, Alabama.

The Institute's programs include bank skills training, drug-abuse prevention, and goal setting. There also is a special program called Pathways to Freedom. It is open to students of all races in kindergarten through twelfth grade. The program gives young people the opportunity to travel across the United States and Canada by bus, tracing the route of the Underground Railroad. The Underground Railroad was a network of people who helped slaves escape to freedom before the Civil War. The Pathways to Freedom program also enables young people to visit places where important civil rights activities occurred. Parks has often accompanied students on these trips.

"Mrs. Parks is a role model that these students look up to," said Elaine Steele, a longtime friend of Parks and cofounder of the Institute. "They feel very honored and privileged to be in her company. And she's very gracious to accompany the students to these activities."

Rosa Parks at a ceremony held in Washington, D.C., in which she received the Congressional Gold Medal, on June 15, 1999.

National Heroine

*A*lthough Parks never attended college, she now has many honorary doctorate degrees, and she has received many awards. A bust of her image is on display at the Smithsonian Institute. In 1994, she received the Rosa Parks Peace Prize in Stockholm, Sweden. In 1996, President Bill Clinton presented her with the Presidential Medal of Freedom. Three years later, he and the U.S. Congress recognized her with the prestigious Congressional Gold Medal.

While signing the bill for the Congressional Gold Medal, Clinton talked to reporters about Parks. "Her action that December day was, in itself, a simple one; but it required uncommon courage," he said. "Rosa Parks's short bus trip, and all the distance she has traveled in the years since, have brought the American people ever closer to the promised land that we know it can truly be."

In December 2000, the people of the city of Montgomery invited Parks to a special ceremony.

The ceremony marked the opening of the Rosa Parks Library and Museum at Troy State University. The museum is a tribute to Parks and the Civil Rights movement. It includes a replica of a 1950s bus that Parks rode the day she was arrested. It also features one of the station wagons used to transport African-Americans during the bus boycott, and a park bench with a life-sized, bronze sculpture of Parks. The library is where the old Empire Theater used to be. It's the very place where Parks refused to give up her seat on the bus.

Despite the credit many give her for sparking the Civil Rights movement, Parks remains modest. She still travels and speaks when she can, and receives many letters from admirers. Parks has written several books. In her book *Quiet Strength*, she remarked, "Four decades later I am still uncomfortable with the credit given to me for starting the bus boycott. I would like [people] to know I was not the only person involved. I was just one of many who fought for freedom."

"To this day, I believe we are here on the planet Earth to live, grow up, and do what we can to make this world a better place for all people to enjoy freedom," she said.

Timeline

1913: Rosa Louise McCauley is born on February 4 in Tuskegee, Alabama.

1955: On December 1, Parks refuses to give up her seat on a Montgomery public bus to a white man. The bus boycott begins, lasting for 381 days.

1963: Dr. Martin Luther King, Jr., gives his famous "I Have a Dream" speech during the March on Washington.

1964: President Lyndon Johnson signs into law the Civil Rights Act.

1965: Civil rights activists march from Selma to Montgomery to protest voting rights abuses.

1987: Parks founds the Rosa and Raymond Parks Institute for Self Development.

1994: Parks is awarded the Rosa Parks Peace Prize in Stockholm, Sweden.

1996: President Bill Clinton presents Parks with the Presidential Medal of Freedom.

1999: The U.S. Congress and President Clinton award Parks the Congressional Gold Medal.

2000: The Rosa Parks Library and Museum at Troy State University opens.

Web Sites

Would you like to learn more about Rosa Parks?
Please visit **www.abdopub.com** to find up-to-date
Web site links about Rosa Parks and the Civil Rights
movement. These links are routinely monitored and
updated to provide the most current information
available.

*Students sit behind a
statue of Rosa Parks
on exhibit at the
National Civil
Rights Museum in
Memphis, Tennessee.*

Glossary

activist
A person who works for political change.

appeal
To take steps to have a case reheard in a higher court.

bail
Money provided to guarantee that a prisoner will show up for his or her trial.

boycott
To refrain from having any dealings with something in order to make a point or change a condition.

Civil Rights movement
The struggle to gain full citizenship rights for African-Americans.

defendant
The party in a lawsuit that is being taken to court.

discriminate
To act on a prejudice, such as a racial prejudice.

establishment

Social, economic, and political leaders who make up a ruling group.

integrate

To bring different groups or races together to live as equals.

National Association for the Advancement of Colored People (NAACP)

An organization founded in 1909 to improve conditions for African-Americans.

plaintiff

The party in a lawsuit that is taking another party to court.

racism

Discrimination against someone based on the belief that his or her race is inferior to another.

segregate

To keep people of different races separate.

unconstitutional

Something that goes against the laws of the U.S. Constitution.

Index

JB
Park

Wheeler, Jill C.
Rosa Parks